CANALS

MAN-MADE WONDERS

Jason Cooper

Rourke Enterprises, Inc.
Vero Beach, Florida 32964

PHOTO CREDITS

© Lynn M. Stone: cover, title page, pages 4, 10, 12, 13, 15, 17, 18, 21;
© Jerry Hennen: page 8; © Frank S. Balthis: page 7

LIBRARY OF CONGRESS
Library of Congress Cataloging-in-Publication Data
Cooper, Jason, 1942-
  Canals / by Jason Cooper.
  p. cm. — (Man made wonders)
  Includes index.
  Summary: Discusses the history and uses of canals and
cites several famous examples.
  ISBN 0-86592-638-7
  1. Canals—Juvenile literature. [1. Canals.]
I. Title. II. Series.
TC745.C66 1991
386'.4—dc20   91-11876
                                         CIP
                                         AC

TABLE OF CONTENTS

CANALS

Water rarely follows the path that people might choose for it. So, for thousands of years, people have dug canals.

Canals are waterways that take water where people want it to go.

Canals serve two main purposes. One purpose is to move ships loaded with passengers or freight. Another purpose is to move water away from wet areas or into dry areas.

Tugboat pushes barges into the lock of a canal

THE FIRST CANALS

Over 4,000 years ago, Egyptians built canals to move river water into the desert. By bringing water to dry land, the Egyptians could plant crops that would not have grown without water.

About 2,500 years ago, the Chinese began to build their Grand Canal. The project took 1,700 years to finish!

The Romans were the first people to build large numbers of canals. Some of their canals were used for **drainage**—the removal of water from places where it was not wanted.

The Grand Canal in China

AMERICA'S EARLY CANALS

The first United States ship canal was built in Massachusetts in 1793. In 1825 the famous Erie Canal was built. It allowed ships in the Atlantic Ocean to reach the Great Lakes.

The Illinois and Michigan Canal opened in 1848. It was just six feet deep, yet it helped turn Chicago into a great city. The canal brought many boat loads of freight to Chicago.

Boats were towed through the old canals by horses and mules walking on a **towpath** next to the canals.

*Mules with a canal boat on the old
Miami and Erie Canal in Ohio*

WATER TRANSPORT CANALS

In wet areas, drainage canals are dug to remove water. In a canal, water flows from one body of water to another one somewhere else.

Draining natural wetlands, such as swamps, is rarely a good idea, however. Swamps and other wetlands are important wild animal homes. They are also places for people to get fresh water.

Irrigation canals carry water to dry lands. The canal water makes the land good for growing crops. Irrigation and drainage canals are often owned by the people who own the land.

A drainage canal

The old Illinois and Michigan Canal, unused for 140 years

Canals make instant waterfront property for backyard boaters in Florida

SHIP CANALS

Ship canals in the United States are planned and operated by the U.S. Army Corps of Engineers.

Ship canals link two or more bodies of water. They allow ships at sea, for example, to reach lakes a long distance away.

Ship canals may be a combination of waterways both natural and man-made. The Atlantic Intracoastal Waterway connects rivers, bays, and canals for hundreds of miles.

The Atlantic and Gulf intracoastal waterways are combinations of canals and natural watercourses

USING A SHIP CANAL

All kinds of ships and pleasure boats use canals. Huge, flat **barges** are often used to ship freight through long canals.

The water level in one part of a canal may be higher than at another part. Canal **locks** are used to lift a ship up or down to the next water level.

Locks are like concrete boxes without tops. They have gates at both ends. After a ship enters a lock, a gate opens to adjust the water level. Then the ship is lifted—or lowered—to the next level.

Barges squeeze into a canal lock after the gate has been opened

FAMOUS CANALS

Ships traveling from New York once had to sail around South America to reach **ports** in California. The Panama Canal changed that when it opened in 1914.

The Panama Canal is a 51-mile ditch through Central America. It connects the Atlantic Ocean with the Pacific Ocean. The Panama Canal took nearly 8,000 miles off the ocean voyage from New York to San Francisco!

The famous Suez Canal is in Egypt. The Chicago Sanitary and Ship Canal connects the Mississippi River to Lake Michigan. The St. Lawrence Seaway opens the Great Lakes to ships from the Atlantic Ocean.

Tugboat guides barges along the Chicago Sanitary and Ship Canal

VENICE: CITY OF CANALS

Venice, Italy, is a city of canals. The city was built long ago on a group of little islands. The people of Venice built a system of transportation using boats and canals.

Today, motorboats have replaced most of Venice's long, wooden boats. However, the canals continue to be the "streets" of Old Venice. And boats are still the city's cars, trucks, and taxis.

Buildings and boats line a canal in Venice, Italy

PROBLEMS WITH CANALS

Big shipping canals can save time and money. But sometimes they create problems, too.

Water animals can use canals to pass from one body of water to another. They may be harmful in their new homes.

The banks of canals may cave in, and soil carried in canal water may begin to fill the canal.

The building of a big ship canal across Florida was stopped even though it had already begun. Building costs were too high and harm to land and wildlife was too great.

Glossary

barge (BARJ) — a flat-bottomed boat for freight, usually pushed or towed by a tugboat on inland waterways

drainage (DRAIN idj) — the process of drawing water away from a place where it is not wanted

irrigation (ear uh GAY shun) — to supply water by human efforts

lock (LAHK) — a chamber with gates at each end used to raise and lower water levels as boats pass from one lock to the next section of a canal

port (PORT) — a city where ships safely dock

towpath (TOE path) — a path from which ships were towed through a canal

INDEX

24

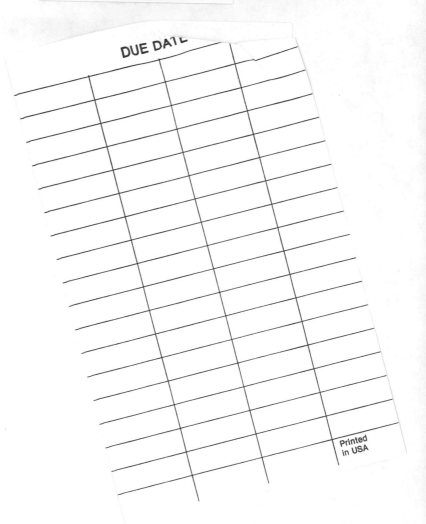

DUE DATE

Printed
in USA